I0440091

# Table Of Contents

# Chapter 1: Introduction to Small Business Tax Deductions

## Understanding the Importance of Tax Deductions for Small Businesses

As a small business owner, you are constantly looking for ways to maximize your profits and minimize your expenses. One area that is often overlooked but can have a significant impact on your bottom line is tax deductions. By understanding the importance of tax deductions and taking advantage of lesser-known deductions, you can potentially save thousands of dollars each year.

Tax deductions are expenses that can be subtracted from your taxable income, reducing the amount of tax you owe. For small businesses, these deductions can include a wide range of expenses, from office supplies and equipment to business travel and advertising costs. By properly tracking and documenting these expenses, you can ensure that you are taking full advantage of all available deductions.

One of the key benefits of tax deductions is that they can help level the playing field for small businesses. Larger corporations often have more resources and can take advantage of a variety of tax loopholes and strategies. However, by understanding and utilizing lesser-known deductions, small businesses can also benefit from significant tax savings.

For example, did you know that as a restaurant owner, you may be able to deduct the cost of uniforms for your employees? Or as a real estate agent, you may be eligible for deductions on your vehicle expenses, such as mileage and maintenance? These are just a few examples of the little-known deductions that can make a big difference for small business owners.

Furthermore, tax deductions can also help you invest in your business and fuel its growth. By reducing your tax liability, you can free up funds to reinvest in marketing, hiring new employees, or expanding your product line. This can ultimately lead to increased profits and a stronger business overall.

However, it is important to note that tax laws are complex and constantly changing. To maximize your deductions and ensure compliance with the law, it is recommended that you consult with a qualified tax professional. They can help you navigate the intricacies of the tax code and identify deductions specific to your industry and niche.

In conclusion, understanding the importance of tax deductions for small businesses is essential for maximizing your profits. By taking advantage of lesser-known deductions, you can significantly reduce your tax liability and free up funds to reinvest in your business. Don't leave money on the table – start exploring the world of tax deductions today and discover how they can benefit your small business.

# How Tax Deductions Can Maximize Your Profits

As a small business owner, you are constantly striving to maximize your profits while minimizing your expenses. One powerful tool at your disposal is tax deductions. By taking advantage of lesser-known tax deductions, you can significantly reduce your tax liability and ultimately increase your bottom line. In this subchapter, we will explore the various ways in which tax deductions can benefit your business, specifically focusing on the lesser-known deductions that many small business owners overlook.

For small businesses, restaurant owners, real estate agents, attorneys, car washes, laundromats, and other niche businesses, understanding these little-known tax deductions can be a game-changer. By identifying and utilizing these deductions, you can keep more of your hard-earned money in your pocket.

In this subchapter, we will delve into a range of tax deductions that are often overlooked by small business owners. We will explore deductions related to operating expenses, business travel, employee benefits, home office deductions, and more. By shedding light on these lesser-known deductions, we aim to provide you with the knowledge and tools to maximize your profits.

Moreover, this subchapter will provide real-life examples and case studies that demonstrate the impact of tax deductions on small businesses. You will learn how to navigate the complex tax code and leverage deductions to your advantage. We will also provide tips on record-keeping and documentation to ensure that you are well-prepared in the event of an audit.

Whether you are a small business owner, a restaurant owner, a real estate agent, an attorney, or in the car wash or laundromat industry, understanding these lesser-known tax deductions can be a game-changer for your business. By optimizing your tax strategy and taking advantage of every available deduction, you can increase your profitability and gain a competitive edge in your industry.

In conclusion, this subchapter aims to empower small business owners with the knowledge and tools to maximize their profits through lesser-known tax deductions. By understanding and utilizing these deductions, you can reduce your tax liability and keep more of your hard-earned money. So, grab a pen and paper, get ready to take notes, and let's dive into the world of little-known small business tax deductions.

# Chapter 2: Commonly Overlooked Tax Deductions for Small Business Owners

## Home Office Deductions: Maximizing Your Savings

As a small business owner, it is crucial to take advantage of every tax deduction available to you. One often overlooked deduction is the home office deduction, which can significantly reduce your tax burden and maximize your savings. In this subchapter, we will explore the ins and outs of home office deductions and provide you with practical tips to ensure you are making the most of this valuable tax benefit.

A home office deduction allows you to deduct expenses related to the space in your home that is exclusively used for your business. This can include a portion of your rent or mortgage, utilities, insurance, and even repairs and maintenance. By accurately calculating and documenting these expenses, you can effectively reduce your overall taxable income and save a substantial amount of money.

To qualify for a home office deduction, you must meet specific requirements set by the Internal Revenue Service (IRS). Your home office must be used regularly and exclusively for your business, meaning it cannot double as a personal space. It should also be your principal place of business, or a place where you meet clients or customers on a regular basis. Furthermore, the space you claim must be clearly delineated and used solely for business purposes.

To maximize your savings through home office deductions, it is crucial to keep detailed records and document all eligible expenses. Create a dedicated space for your home office and maintain it in a professional manner. Keep track of all expenses related to your office, such as receipts for furniture, equipment, and supplies. Additionally, document your utility bills and mortgage or rent payments, clearly indicating the portion that corresponds to your office space.

It is also important to stay updated on any changes to tax laws and regulations regarding home office deductions. The IRS frequently updates its guidelines, so familiarize yourself with the latest requirements to ensure you are taking full advantage of this deduction. Consulting with a tax professional who specializes in small business deductions can also provide valuable insights and help you navigate the complexities of tax regulations.

In conclusion, home office deductions offer a fantastic opportunity for small business owners to maximize their savings. By understanding the requirements and diligently tracking your expenses, you can significantly reduce your taxable income and keep more money in your pocket. Don't overlook this valuable deduction – start maximizing your savings today!

## Transportation and Travel Expenses: Making Every Mile Count

As a small business owner, it is vital to stay on top of your expenses and find every possible tax deduction available to you. One area that is often overlooked is transportation and travel expenses. By maximizing these deductions, you can significantly reduce your tax liability and increase your profits. In this subchapter, we will explore the lesser-known tax deductions related to transportation and travel that can benefit small businesses across various industries.

For small businesses, restaurant owners, real estate agents, attorneys, car washes, and laundromats, transportation and travel expenses are often a significant part of their operations. Whether it is delivering goods, meeting clients, attending conferences, or visiting different locations, every mile counts when it comes to tax deductions.

One important tax deduction to consider is the standard mileage rate. The IRS allows you to deduct a certain amount per mile for business-related driving. This deduction covers not only fuel expenses but also wear and tear on your vehicle. Keeping detailed records of your business-related mileage is crucial for claiming this deduction accurately.

For businesses in the food and hospitality industry, travel expenses related to attending industry events, conferences, or visiting suppliers can also be deducted. These expenses include transportation, lodging, and meals. By attending such events, you not only gain valuable knowledge and networking opportunities but also reap the benefits of tax deductions.

Real estate agents, attorneys, and other professionals who frequently travel to meet clients or visit properties can also take advantage of transportation and travel deductions. Expenses such as airfare, hotel accommodations, rental cars, and meals can be deducted if they are directly related to your business activities. Additionally, if you use your personal vehicle for business purposes, you can deduct the actual expenses incurred, including gas, repairs, insurance, and depreciation.

Car washes and laundromats can also benefit from transportation deductions. If you provide a pickup and delivery service for your customers, the expenses related to these trips can be deducted. This includes fuel, vehicle maintenance, and even the cost of hiring drivers if applicable.

In conclusion, transportation and travel expenses are often overlooked but can be a significant source of tax deductions for small businesses in various industries. By keeping detailed records and understanding the specific deductions available to your business, you can maximize your profits and reduce your tax liability. Remember, every mile counts, so make sure to take advantage of these lesser-known tax deductions and keep your business thriving.

## Equipment and Supplies: Deducting Essential Business Assets

As a small business owner, you are constantly striving to maximize your profits and minimize your expenses. One area that often goes overlooked is the potential tax deductions available for your essential business assets. In this subchapter, we will explore the lesser-known tax deductions that can greatly benefit small businesses, restaurant owners, real estate agents, attorneys, car washes, and laundromats.

When it comes to equipment and supplies, the IRS allows you to deduct the cost of items that are necessary for running your business. This includes everything from office equipment and furniture to kitchen appliances and cleaning supplies. By taking advantage of these deductions, you can significantly reduce your taxable income and save money on your tax bill.

For small businesses, investing in equipment is often a significant expense. However, the good news is that these purchases can be fully deducted in the year they were bought, thanks to the Section 179 deduction. This deduction allows you to deduct the full cost of qualifying equipment, up to a certain limit, rather than depreciating the cost over several years. This can provide a substantial boost to your bottom line and help you reinvest in your business sooner rather than later.

Restaurant owners, in particular, can benefit greatly from this deduction. From commercial ovens and grills to refrigerators and dishwashers, the cost of restaurant equipment can quickly add up. By taking advantage of the Section 179 deduction, you can free up funds to invest in other areas of your restaurant, such as marketing or staff training.

Real estate agents, attorneys, car washes, and laundromats also rely heavily on equipment and supplies to operate efficiently. Whether it's cameras and computers for real estate agents, legal software and office furniture for attorneys, or washing machines and dryers for car washes and laundromats, these assets are essential to their respective businesses. By deducting these expenses, they can reduce their tax liability and allocate more resources towards growing their businesses.

In conclusion, understanding and utilizing the lesser-known tax deductions for equipment and supplies can be a game-changer for small businesses, restaurant owners, real estate agents, attorneys, car washes, and laundromats. By taking advantage of the Section 179 deduction and deducting the cost of these essential assets, you can maximize your profits and keep more money in your pocket. So, make sure to consult with a tax professional to ensure you are taking full advantage of these deductions and saving as much as possible come tax time.

## Marketing and Advertising Costs: Promoting Your Business Tax-efficiently

In today's competitive marketplace, marketing and advertising play a crucial role in the success of any business. However, the costs associated with promoting your business can quickly add up and become a significant burden on your bottom line. As a small business owner, it is essential to explore every avenue to maximize your profits and minimize your expenses. Fortunately, there are several lesser-known tax deductions available to small business owners that can help offset your marketing and advertising costs.

One of the most effective tax deductions for promoting your business is the deduction for ordinary and necessary business expenses. This includes costs such as print and online advertisements, billboards, radio or television commercials, and even website design and maintenance. By properly documenting these expenses and ensuring they are directly related to your business, you can deduct them from your taxable income, ultimately reducing your overall tax liability.

Another tax-efficient way to promote your business is by utilizing social media platforms. Many small business owners underestimate the power of social media in reaching a broader audience at a fraction of the cost of traditional advertising methods. The expenses incurred in running social media campaigns, including content creation, paid ads, and analytics tools, can also be deducted as ordinary and necessary business expenses.

If you host events or sponsor local community activities to promote your business, you may be eligible for tax deductions as well. Expenses related to organizing trade shows, sponsoring charity events, or hosting seminars can be deducted, provided they are directly related to your business and aimed at promoting it.

Furthermore, as a restaurant owner, real estate agent, attorney, car wash, or laundromat owner, you can take advantage of industry-specific tax deductions. For instance, restaurant owners can deduct the costs of menu design, food photography, and even the expenses incurred in participating in food festivals or competitions. Real estate agents can deduct expenses related to property listings, staging, and professional photography. Attorneys can deduct expenses related to legal directories, professional memberships, and even legal research software. Similarly, car washes and laundromats can deduct expenses associated with signage, equipment maintenance, and even the costs of developing loyalty programs.

In conclusion, by understanding and utilizing the lesser-known tax deductions available to small business owners, you can significantly reduce the financial burden of marketing and advertising costs. Properly documenting and categorizing your expenses, whether they are related to traditional advertising methods, social media campaigns, or industry-specific promotions, can help maximize your profits and minimize your tax liability. By taking advantage of these tax deductions, you can ensure that your business thrives in a tax-efficient manner, allowing you to focus on what you do best – serving your customers and growing your business.

# Professional Services: Leveraging Deductible Expertise

In the world of small business ownership, maximizing profits is always a top priority. As a business owner, you are constantly on the lookout for ways to minimize expenses and increase your bottom line. One often overlooked area where small business owners can save money is in professional services. By leveraging deductible expertise, you can unlock a wealth of tax deductions that can significantly impact your annual tax liability.

For small businesses, restaurant owners, real estate agents, attorneys, car washes, laundromats, and other niche industries, understanding the lesser-known tax deductions available to you can be a game-changer. This subchapter aims to shed light on these little-known small business tax deductions and how you can leverage professional services to maximize your profits.

One of the key aspects of leveraging deductible expertise is to engage the services of qualified professionals who specialize in tax planning and accounting. These professionals have an in-depth understanding of the tax code and can help identify deductions specific to your industry. Whether it's a tax consultant, accountant, or tax attorney, their expertise can save you time, money, and potential headaches.

In the restaurant industry, for example, you may not be aware that the cost of menu development, recipe testing, and even staff training can be tax-deductible expenses. By working with a knowledgeable tax consultant, you can ensure that these expenses are properly documented and claimed.

Real estate agents, on the other hand, can benefit from deducting marketing expenses, home office expenses, and even mileage when showing properties. By consulting with a tax professional experienced in the real estate industry, you can uncover deductions that may have been missed in the past.

Attorneys, car washes, and laundromats also have unique deductions available to them. Legal research fees, maintenance costs, and utility expenses can all be deductible for attorneys. Car washes can often claim deductions for equipment maintenance and water usage, while laundromats may be eligible for deductions on commercial laundry equipment and repairs.

In conclusion, understanding and leveraging deductible expertise within professional services is a vital step in maximizing your profits as a small business owner. By working with qualified professionals who specialize in tax planning and accounting, you can identify and claim the lesser-known tax deductions specific to your industry. Don't leave money on the table – take advantage of professional services to reduce your tax liability and increase your bottom line.

# Startup Costs: Navigating the Initial Investment

Starting a new business venture can be an exciting but daunting endeavor. One of the crucial aspects that entrepreneurs must carefully consider is the initial investment required to get their business off the ground. This subchapter aims to guide small business owners, including restaurant owners, real estate agents, attorneys, car washes, and laundromats, through the process of managing startup costs effectively. By uncovering lesser-known tax deductions, this information will help maximize profits and alleviate financial burdens.

When embarking on a new business venture, it is essential to understand the concept of startup costs. These are the expenses incurred before your business begins generating revenue, such as market research, legal fees, advertising, and initial inventory. Many entrepreneurs are unaware that certain startup costs can be deducted from their taxes, reducing their overall financial burden.

Under the United States tax code, small business owners can take advantage of various tax deductions specifically designed to support startups. For instance, the cost of market research and feasibility studies can be deducted as business expenses. Additionally, legal and professional fees incurred during the startup phase, including those for consulting and accounting services, can also be deducted.

Furthermore, this subchapter explores unique tax deductions available to specific niches. For restaurant owners, costs associated with menu development, staff training, and even food tastings can potentially be deducted. Real estate agents can learn about deductions for advertising expenses, MLS fees, and even mileage when showing properties. Attorneys can find valuable information on deducting legal research, bar association dues, and professional memberships. Car wash owners can learn about deductions for equipment purchases, maintenance costs, and even water and utility bills. Lastly, laundromat owners can uncover deductions for machine maintenance, detergent expenses, and even security measures.

By understanding and utilizing these little-known tax deductions, small business owners can significantly reduce their startup costs and maximize their profits. Remember, it is crucial to keep detailed records of all expenses and consult with a tax professional to ensure compliance with tax regulations and take full advantage of available deductions. With proper knowledge and planning, navigating the initial investment can become a more manageable task, allowing entrepreneurs to focus on building a successful business.

## Education and Training Expenses: Expanding Your Knowledge, Reducing Your Taxes

In the competitive world of small business ownership, staying ahead of the curve is key to success. As a small business owner, you know that knowledge is power and that continually expanding your skillset is essential for growth. The good news is that not only can you enhance your expertise, but you can also reduce your tax burden through education and training expenses. In this subchapter, we will explore the lesser-known tax deductions available to small business owners, including restaurant owners, real estate agents, attorneys, car washes, and laundromats, to help you maximize your profits.

One of the most valuable deductions you may be overlooking is the cost of educational courses and workshops directly related to your business. Whether you are a restaurant owner looking to learn the latest culinary trends, a real estate agent aiming to stay updated on market dynamics, an attorney seeking specialized legal training, or a car wash or laundromat owner interested in new cleaning techniques, the expenses incurred for these educational endeavors can be fully deductible.

Furthermore, the cost of industry-specific conferences, seminars, and trade shows can also be claimed as deductions. Attending these events not only provides you with networking opportunities but also allows you to stay current with the latest industry trends and innovations. By deducting these expenses, you are essentially investing in your business's growth while simultaneously reducing your taxable income.

It's important to note that the IRS requires the education or training to be directly related to your business or to maintain or improve skills necessary for your business. Therefore, it is crucial to keep records of your attendance, receipts, and any other relevant documentation to substantiate your claim.

Remember, as a small business owner, your success depends on your ability to adapt and grow. By taking advantage of these lesser-known tax deductions for education and training expenses, you are investing not only in yourself but also in the long-term success of your business. So, continue expanding your knowledge, enhancing your skills, and reducing your taxes to maximize your profits and stay ahead in your industry.

# Chapter 3: Industry-Specific Tax Deductions

## Restaurant Owners: Deducting Food and Beverage Expenses

Restaurant owners have a lot on their plate, and one often overlooked area where they can maximize their profits is by taking advantage of tax deductions for food and beverage expenses. In this subchapter, we will explore the lesser-known tax deductions available to small business owners in the restaurant industry.

One of the most significant deductions for restaurant owners is the cost of raw materials, including food and beverages. Whether you run a fine dining establishment or a casual eatery, you can deduct the cost of ingredients used to prepare meals and drinks. This deduction can help reduce your taxable income and ultimately increase your profits.

Additionally, restaurant owners can deduct the costs of non-alcoholic beverages served to customers. Whether you offer complimentary water, soft drinks, or specialty beverages, these expenses can be written off as a business expense. However, it's important to keep detailed records and receipts to substantiate these deductions during an audit.

Another often overlooked deduction is the cost of samples or tastings provided to potential customers. If you offer free samples to attract new patrons or hold wine tastings to promote your restaurant, you can deduct the cost of these samples as a marketing expense. This deduction not only helps boost your bottom line but also encourages you to invest in promotional activities to attract new customers.

Restaurant owners can also deduct the cost of uniforms and protective clothing for employees. Whether it's chef coats, aprons, or hairnets, these expenses can be deducted as a business expense. It's important to note that the clothing must be mandatory and bear the company logo or be specific to the restaurant industry.

Lastly, if your restaurant offers delivery services, you can deduct expenses related to delivery vehicles, fuel, and maintenance. These costs can add up quickly, so it's crucial to keep accurate records and receipts to support your deductions.

In conclusion, restaurant owners have several lesser-known tax deductions available to them that can help maximize their profits. From deducting the cost of raw materials and non-alcoholic beverages to marketing expenses for samples and tastings, taking advantage of these deductions can significantly reduce your taxable income. Additionally, deducting the cost of uniforms and protective clothing, as well as delivery expenses, can further enhance your financial position. As a small business owner in the restaurant industry, it's essential to stay informed about these lesser-known deductions to ensure you are maximizing your profits and minimizing your tax liability.

# Real Estate Agents: Capitalizing on Deductions in the Housing Market

In the highly competitive real estate market, every dollar counts. As a real estate agent, you need to be aware of every possible deduction that can help you maximize your profits and reduce your tax burden. This subchapter will delve into the little-known tax deductions specifically tailored for small business owners in the real estate sector.

One significant deduction that real estate agents often overlook is the home office deduction. If you use a portion of your home exclusively for your real estate business, you may be eligible to deduct expenses related to that space. This includes a portion of your rent or mortgage interest, utilities, insurance, and even depreciation. However, it is important to ensure that your home office meets the IRS criteria to qualify for this deduction.

Another deduction to take advantage of is the automobile expenses. As a real estate agent, you spend a significant amount of time driving to properties, meetings, and showings. Keep track of your mileage and other vehicle-related expenses, such as gas, repairs, and insurance. These expenses can be deducted either using the standard mileage rate or by calculating the actual expenses.

Marketing and advertising costs are also deductible for real estate agents. Whether it's printed materials, online advertisements, or hosting an open house, these expenses can add up quickly. Be sure to keep detailed records of all your marketing expenses, as they can significantly reduce your taxable income.

Furthermore, real estate agents often incur expenses for professional development and continuing education. Whether you attend seminars, conferences, or workshops to enhance your skills and knowledge, these expenses can be deducted. Additionally, fees paid to professional organizations and subscriptions to industry-specific publications are also deductible.

Lastly, don't forget about the deductions related to technology and software expenses. As a real estate agent, you rely heavily on technology to manage your listings, communicate with clients, and market your properties. Expenses for computers, smartphones, software subscriptions, and website development can all be deducted.

In conclusion, real estate agents have several lesser-known tax deductions available to them. By capitalizing on these deductions, you can reduce your tax liability and maximize your profits. Remember to consult with a tax professional or CPA to ensure you are taking full advantage of all the deductions available to you as a small business owner in the real estate industry.

## Attorneys: Maximizing Deductions in the Legal Profession

As an attorney, you provide essential legal services to your clients, but did you know that there are numerous tax deductions available to help maximize your profits? In this subchapter, we will explore the lesser-known tax deductions specifically tailored to the legal profession. By taking advantage of these deductions, you can optimize your financial situation and keep more money in your pocket.

One crucial deduction for attorneys is the home office deduction. If you have a dedicated space in your home that is exclusively used for your legal practice, you may be eligible to deduct a portion of your home expenses, such as rent or mortgage interest, utilities, and insurance. This deduction can significantly reduce your overall tax liability.

Additionally, maintaining and upgrading your law library is a necessary expense for any attorney. Fortunately, these costs can be deducted as well. Whether you purchase legal books, subscribe to online legal research platforms, or attend seminars and workshops to stay updated on the latest legal developments, you can deduct these expenses as necessary business costs.

Another often overlooked deduction is professional association fees. As an attorney, joining bar associations and professional organizations is not only beneficial for networking and professional development but also tax-deductible. Don't forget to include the cost of your membership dues when filing your taxes.

Furthermore, continuing legal education (CLE) courses and seminars are essential for staying up-to-date with the ever-evolving legal landscape. Fortunately, these expenses can be claimed as deductions, ensuring that you can maintain your expertise while minimizing your tax burden.

Finally, don't forget about the deductions related to business-related travel and entertainment expenses. As an attorney, you may frequently need to travel to meet clients, attend court hearings, or engage in settlement negotiations. Keep track of your travel expenses, including airfare, hotel accommodations, meals, and even parking fees. Additionally, if you entertain clients or potential clients, a portion of those expenses can be deducted as well.

In conclusion, as an attorney, you have unique opportunities to maximize your deductions and increase your profitability. By taking advantage of deductions such as home office expenses, law library costs, professional association fees, CLE courses, and business travel and entertainment expenses, you can reduce your tax liability and keep more money in your pocket. Stay informed about these lesser-known tax deductions and consult with a tax professional to ensure you are making the most of your legal profession.

# Car Washes: Expensing Equipment and Utility Costs

One of the most significant expenses for car wash businesses is the purchase and maintenance of equipment. From high-pressure hoses to automated cleaning systems, the cost of these essential tools can quickly add up. However, did you know that you may be eligible to deduct these expenses from your taxes? In this subchapter, we will explore the tax benefits available to car wash owners and how you can maximize your profits by taking advantage of lesser-known tax deductions.

When it comes to equipment purchases, the IRS allows small businesses to deduct the full cost of qualifying equipment in the year of purchase under Section 179 of the tax code. This means that instead of depreciating the equipment over several years, you can deduct the entire expense upfront, reducing your taxable income. For car wash owners, this deduction can be a significant financial advantage, as it allows you to invest in new and improved equipment while minimizing your tax liability.

Additionally, car washes also incur substantial utility costs, primarily electricity and water. These expenses are necessary for the day-to-day operations of your business, but they can also be deductible. By keeping accurate records of your utility bills, you can claim a deduction for the portion of these costs that are directly related to your car wash operations. This includes the electricity used to power your equipment and the water consumed during the cleaning process.

It is crucial for small business owners, including car washes, to be aware of these lesser-known tax deductions. By taking advantage of these tax benefits, you can significantly reduce your tax burden and increase your overall profitability. However, it is essential to consult with a tax professional or accountant who specializes in small business tax deductions to ensure you are maximizing your benefits while staying compliant with the tax laws.

In conclusion, car washes can benefit greatly from expensing equipment and utility costs when it comes to tax deductions. By understanding the tax code and staying informed about the available deductions, you can make strategic decisions that not only improve your car wash operations but also maximize your profits. Remember, investing in new equipment and tracking your utility costs can be financially advantageous, so be sure to explore these deductions and keep your business on the path to success.

## Laundromats: Deducting Maintenance and Utility Expenses

Running a successful laundromat business involves more than just washing and drying clothes. As a small business owner in the laundry industry, it is crucial to understand the various tax deductions that can help you maximize your profits. One such deduction that often goes unnoticed is the deduction for maintenance and utility expenses.

Maintenance expenses refer to the costs incurred to keep your laundromat in good working condition. This includes routine repairs, equipment maintenance, and any necessary upgrades or replacements. The good news is that these expenses can be deducted from your business income, ultimately reducing your tax liability.

To ensure that you can claim these deductions, it is essential to keep accurate records of all maintenance-related expenses. This includes invoices, receipts, and any other relevant documentation. By doing so, you can substantiate your claims and provide the necessary evidence in case of an audit.

Additionally, utility expenses can also be deducted as business expenses. Laundromats typically have high utility bills due to the constant operation of washers, dryers, and other equipment. These expenses can quickly add up, making it crucial to take advantage of the tax benefits they offer.

When deducting utility expenses, it is important to differentiate between personal and business use. If you have an on-site office or staff area, only deduct the portion of the utility expenses that relate to the operational areas of your laundromat. This can be calculated based on square footage or the actual time spent operating the business.

To simplify the process of claiming maintenance and utility deductions, it is recommended to work with a qualified tax professional who specializes in small business tax deductions. They can help you navigate the complex tax laws and ensure that you take advantage of all the deductions available to you.

In conclusion, as a laundromat owner, you have the opportunity to reduce your tax liability by deducting maintenance and utility expenses. By keeping meticulous records, accurately separating personal and business use, and seeking professional advice, you can maximize your profits and minimize your tax burden. Remember, every dollar saved through tax deductions is a dollar that can be reinvested in your business's growth and success.

# Chapter 4: Advanced Strategies for Optimizing Tax Deductions

## Tax Credits: Unlocking Extra Savings

As a small business owner, you are likely aware of the numerous tax deductions available to you. However, what if we told you that there are even more ways to save on your taxes that you may not be aware of? Welcome to the world of tax credits – a lesser-known avenue to unlock extra savings for your business.

Tax credits are powerful tools that can significantly reduce your tax liability, sometimes even dollar-for-dollar. Unlike tax deductions that lower your taxable income, tax credits directly reduce the amount of tax you owe. These credits can make a substantial difference in your bottom line, allowing you to keep more of your hard-earned profits.

One valuable tax credit that small businesses should explore is the Research and Development (R&D) Tax Credit. Contrary to popular belief, this credit is not limited to tech companies or laboratories. Whether you are a restaurant owner experimenting with new recipes or a real estate agent developing innovative marketing strategies, if you are investing time and money into improving your business processes, you may qualify for this credit.

Another credit often overlooked is the Work Opportunity Tax Credit (WOTC). This credit rewards businesses that hire individuals from specific targeted groups, such as veterans, long-term unemployed, or individuals receiving government assistance. By hiring from these groups, you not only contribute to the community but also enjoy a tax credit that can be a significant financial benefit.

Moreover, if you are an attorney, you may be eligible for the Domestic Production Activities Deduction (DPAD). This credit incentivizes businesses engaged in manufacturing, production, or construction activities within the United States. Many legal practices often overlook this credit, assuming it is solely for traditional manufacturing businesses. However, if your firm engages in any qualifying activities, you should explore the potential savings offered by the DPAD.

Car washes and laundromats can also benefit from tax credits, such as the Energy Efficiency Tax Credit. By investing in energy-efficient equipment or making improvements to reduce energy consumption, you can not only save on your utility bills but also enjoy a tax credit for your eco-friendly initiatives.

In conclusion, as a small business owner, it is crucial to be aware of the lesser-known tax credits that can unlock extra savings for your business. By exploring options like the R&D Tax Credit, WOTC, DPAD, or Energy Efficiency Tax Credit, you can potentially reduce your tax liability and maximize your profits. Don't miss out on these opportunities to optimize your tax strategy and keep more money in your pocket.

# Section 179: Accelerating Deductions for Business Assets

In the world of small business ownership, every dollar counts. As a small business owner, you are constantly seeking ways to maximize your profits and minimize your tax liabilities. One lesser-known tax deduction that can significantly benefit your bottom line is Section 179.

Section 179 of the Internal Revenue Code allows businesses to deduct the full purchase price of qualifying equipment and software purchased or financed during the tax year. This deduction is especially beneficial for small businesses, restaurant owners, real estate agents, attorneys, car washes, and laundromats.

Under Section 179, you can deduct the full cost of qualifying assets up to a certain limit, rather than depreciating them over several years. This means that you can accelerate your deductions and reduce your taxable income immediately, providing a powerful tool to boost your cash flow.

The types of assets that qualify for Section 179 deductions are broad and include tangible personal property, such as machinery, equipment, vehicles, and furniture, as well as off-the-shelf software. Additionally, certain improvements to non-residential real estate, such as roofs, heating, ventilation, and air conditioning systems, can also qualify for this deduction.

The current maximum deduction limit for Section 179 is $1,050,000 for the tax year 2022. However, it's important to note that this limit is subject to a phase-out threshold of $2,620,000. Once your total investment in qualifying assets exceeds this threshold, the deduction begins to reduce on a dollar-for-dollar basis until it is fully phased out.

One significant advantage of Section 179 is that it can be used for both new and used equipment. This flexibility allows small businesses to take advantage of cost-effective options in acquiring necessary assets while still enjoying the benefits of accelerated depreciation.

To claim the Section 179 deduction, you must use IRS Form 4562 and attach it to your tax return. It's crucial to keep accurate records of your purchases and consult with a tax professional to ensure you meet all the necessary requirements.

In conclusion, Section 179 offers a valuable opportunity for small businesses, restaurant owners, real estate agents, attorneys, car washes, and laundromats to maximize their tax deductions. By accelerating deductions for business assets, you can reduce your taxable income, improve cash flow, and ultimately maximize your profits. Don't overlook this lesser-known tax deduction – it could make a significant difference in your bottom line.

## Retirement Contributions: Reducing Taxes while Securing Your Future

In the fast-paced world of small business ownership, it's easy to get caught up in the day-to-day operations and overlook the importance of planning for your future. However, by making strategic retirement contributions, you can not only reduce your tax burden but also secure a financially stable future for yourself and your business.

As a small business owner, you have access to a range of retirement plans that offer significant tax advantages. By taking advantage of these lesser-known tax deductions, you can maximize your profits while ensuring a comfortable retirement.

One popular retirement plan option for small businesses is the Simplified Employee Pension (SEP) IRA. With a SEP IRA, you can contribute up to 25% of your net self-employment income, up to a maximum of $58,000 (as of 2021). These contributions are tax-deductible, meaning you can lower your taxable income while saving for retirement.

Another option is the Solo 401(k) plan, also known as an Individual 401(k). Designed for self-employed individuals without employees, this plan allows for both employee and employer contributions. As the business owner, you can contribute up to $19,500 as an employee (plus an additional $6,500 if you're over 50), and you can also contribute up to 25% of your net self-employment income as the employer, up to a combined maximum of $58,000 (as of 2021). These contributions are tax-deductible, providing you with substantial tax savings.

Real estate agents, attorneys, and other professionals can take advantage of the defined benefit pension plan, which allows for significantly higher contribution limits. With this plan, you can contribute an amount that will provide a predetermined benefit in retirement, based on factors such as your age, income, and years of service. The contributions are tax-deductible, and the plan can be tailored to meet your specific retirement needs.

By making retirement contributions, you not only reduce your taxable income in the present but also benefit from tax-deferred growth on your investments. This can result in substantial savings over time and provide you with a nest egg to rely on when you decide to retire.

In conclusion, as a small business owner, it's crucial to prioritize your retirement contributions. By taking advantage of lesser-known tax deductions, such as SEP IRAs, Solo 401(k) plans, and defined benefit pension plans, you can reduce your tax burden while securing your financial future. Don't wait until it's too late – start planning for retirement today and maximize your profits for years to come.

# Health Insurance Deductions: Managing Healthcare Costs

In today's competitive business landscape, managing healthcare costs is a critical aspect of running a successful small business. As a small business owner, you understand the importance of providing health insurance benefits to attract and retain top talent, but the associated costs can often be overwhelming. Fortunately, there are lesser-known tax deductions available that can help you maximize your profits and alleviate some of the financial burden.

One of the most valuable deductions for small business owners is related to health insurance premiums. Under the current tax code, you can deduct the cost of health insurance premiums paid for yourself, your employees, and their dependents. This deduction can significantly reduce your taxable income, resulting in substantial savings.

To qualify for this deduction, you must meet certain criteria. First, your business must be classified as a sole proprietorship, partnership,

LLC, or S corporation. Additionally, the health insurance plan must be established under your business name. If you are a self-employed individual, you may also be eligible for a deduction for your personal health insurance premiums.

It's important to note that the deduction for health insurance premiums is an above-the-line deduction, meaning you can claim it even if you do not itemize deductions on your tax return. This is a significant advantage for small business owners who may not have enough eligible expenses to justify itemizing deductions.

Furthermore, small businesses with fewer than 25 full-time equivalent employees may qualify for an additional tax credit known as the Small Business Health Care Tax Credit. This credit is specifically designed to assist small businesses in providing health insurance coverage to their employees. By taking advantage of this credit, you can further reduce the overall cost of healthcare for your business.

As a small business owner, it is crucial to explore all available tax deductions to maximize your profits and effectively manage healthcare costs. By leveraging the deduction for health insurance premiums and potentially qualifying for the Small Business Health Care Tax Credit, you can minimize the financial impact of providing healthcare benefits to your employees.

In conclusion, health insurance deductions are a valuable tool for small business owners in managing healthcare costs. By understanding the specific criteria and taking advantage of available tax credits, you can ensure that your business remains competitive while minimizing the financial strain. As you navigate the complexities of small business tax deductions, it is advisable to consult with a qualified tax professional who can provide personalized guidance tailored to your unique circumstances.

# Self-Employment Tax Deductions: Lowering Your Tax Liability

As a small business owner, you understand the importance of maximizing your profits and minimizing your tax liability. While most entrepreneurs are familiar with common deductions such as office expenses and employee salaries, there are several lesser-known tax deductions specifically tailored for small business owners like you. In this subchapter, we will explore some little-known small business tax deductions that can help you significantly lower your tax liability.

One of the key areas where small business owners can benefit from tax deductions is in self-employment taxes. Unlike employees who have their Social Security and Medicare taxes withheld from their paychecks, self-employed individuals are responsible for paying these taxes themselves. However, there are several deductions you can claim to reduce your self-employment tax liability.

Firstly, you can deduct the employer portion of the self-employment tax. As a self-employed individual, you are both the employer and the employee, which means you are responsible for paying both portions of the Social Security and Medicare taxes. However, you can deduct the employer portion of these taxes, effectively reducing your overall self-employment tax liability.

Additionally, you can deduct the cost of health insurance premiums. If you are self-employed and pay for your own health insurance, you can deduct the premiums as an adjustment to your income. This deduction not only lowers your self-employment tax liability but also reduces your overall taxable income.

Furthermore, if you contribute to a retirement plan such as a Simplified Employee Pension (SEP) IRA or a solo 401(k), you can deduct your contributions from your self-employment income. This deduction not only helps you save for retirement but also reduces your self-employment tax liability.

Finally, keep in mind that business-related expenses can also be deducted from your self-employment income. This includes expenses such as office supplies, advertising costs, professional fees, and business travel expenses. By carefully tracking and documenting these expenses, you can lower your self-employment tax liability while ensuring your business operates efficiently.

In conclusion, understanding and utilizing self-employment tax deductions can significantly reduce your tax liability as a small business owner. By deducting the employer portion of the self-employment tax, health insurance premiums, retirement contributions, and business-related expenses, you can maximize your profits and keep more of your hard-earned money. Stay informed, consult with a tax professional, and take advantage of these lesser-known deductions to ensure your business thrives financially.

# Chapter 5: Record-Keeping and Documentation for Small Business Tax Deductions

## Organizing Your Financial Records: The Key to Successful Deductions

In the fast-paced world of small business ownership, staying on top of your finances is crucial. As a small business owner, you are likely always on the lookout for ways to reduce your tax burden and maximize your profits. One often overlooked strategy is taking advantage of lesser-known tax deductions. To fully benefit from these deductions, however, it is essential to have an organized system for managing your financial records.

Properly organizing your financial records can make a world of difference when it comes to maximizing your deductions. By keeping accurate and up-to-date records, you can ensure that you never miss out on a potential tax deduction. Whether you are a restaurant owner, real estate agent, attorney, car wash, or laundromat owner, implementing a solid record-keeping system is essential.

First and foremost, consider using accounting software or hiring a professional bookkeeper to help streamline your financial record-keeping process. These tools can assist you in tracking your income and expenses, generating financial reports, and ensuring that your records are accurate and complete. By having well-organized financial statements, you can easily identify deductible expenses and provide the necessary documentation during tax season.

Another important aspect of organizing your financial records is separating personal and business expenses. Mixing personal and business finances can lead to confusion and potential audit triggers. Establish separate bank accounts and credit cards specifically for your business. This separation not only helps with record-keeping but also demonstrates to the IRS that you are treating your business as a separate entity.

In addition, it is crucial to maintain proper documentation for all your business expenses. Keep receipts, invoices, and any other relevant documents that support your claimed deductions. This includes expenses such as office supplies, marketing and advertising costs, professional fees, travel expenses, and more. By having detailed records, you can substantiate your deductions and ensure compliance with IRS regulations.

Remember, organizing your financial records is an ongoing process. Set aside time each week or month to review and update your records. Regularly reconciling your bank and credit card statements will help catch any discrepancies and ensure accuracy.

In conclusion, organizing your financial records is the key to successfully maximizing your deductions as a small business owner. By implementing a solid record-keeping system, you can identify and claim lesser-known tax deductions, reducing your overall tax liability and increasing your profits. Whether you are a restaurant owner, real estate agent, attorney, car wash, or laundromat owner, take the time to establish an organized approach to managing your financial records – it will pay off in the long run.

# Tracking Expenses and Income: Efficient Systems for Small Business Owners

In the fast-paced world of small business ownership, it is crucial for entrepreneurs to have efficient systems in place to track their expenses and income. By implementing effective tracking methods, small business owners can gain a comprehensive understanding of their financial health, maximize their profits, and take advantage of lesser-known tax deductions. This subchapter aims to provide valuable insights and techniques to help businesses in various niches, including restaurants, real estate agents, attorneys, car washes, and laundromats, optimize their financial management.

One of the first steps towards efficient expense tracking is to establish a dedicated system for recording all business-related expenditures. This can be accomplished through the use of accounting software or even simple spreadsheets. By diligently logging each expense, whether it be office supplies, utilities, or employee wages, small business owners can accurately monitor their cash flow and identify areas where costs can be reduced or eliminated.

In addition to tracking expenses, it is equally important for small business owners to keep a close eye on their income. Implementing a streamlined system to record all sources of revenue, such as sales, services rendered, or rental income, allows for a clear understanding of the financial health of the business. By regularly reconciling income with expenses, owners can identify any discrepancies or potential issues before they become major problems.

Furthermore, this subchapter will delve into the lesser-known tax deductions available to small business owners. By understanding and leveraging these deductions, entrepreneurs can potentially save thousands of dollars annually. For example, restaurant owners may be eligible for deductions related to food and beverage costs, while real estate agents can take advantage of deductions for advertising and marketing expenses. Attorneys may discover deductions related to legal research materials, and car washes and laundromats can explore deductions for equipment maintenance and repair.

In conclusion, tracking expenses and income efficiently is essential for small business owners in various niches to maximize their profits and take advantage of lesser-known tax deductions. By implementing dedicated systems for expense and income tracking, entrepreneurs can gain valuable insights into their financial health, identify areas for improvement, and potentially save on taxes. Whether you own a restaurant, real estate agency, law firm, car wash, or laundromat, this subchapter will provide you with the tools and knowledge necessary to optimize your financial management and ultimately maximize your profits.

## Record-Keeping Best Practices: Staying Compliant with the IRS

One of the most crucial aspects of running a small business is staying compliant with the Internal Revenue Service (IRS). As a small business owner, it is your responsibility to maintain accurate records of your financial transactions and expenses. This not only ensures that you are in good standing with the IRS but also allows you to take advantage of lesser-known tax deductions that can maximize your profits. In this subchapter, we will explore record-keeping best practices that will help you stay compliant with the IRS and discover those hidden tax deductions.

Accurate and organized record-keeping is the foundation of any successful small business. It is crucial to keep track of all income and expenses, including receipts, invoices, bank statements, and any other relevant financial documents. Maintaining a separate business bank account is highly recommended, as it streamlines the process and avoids mixing personal and business expenses.

Implementing a reliable system for record-keeping is essential. This can be as simple as using spreadsheets or investing in accounting software that automates the process. Regularly updating your records, ideally on a weekly or monthly basis, ensures that you have an up-to-date and accurate view of your financials.

One aspect that many small business owners overlook is the importance of documenting any changes or updates in their business structure. For example, if you are a restaurant owner who recently added a catering service to your business, it is crucial to update your records accordingly. This will help you accurately calculate and claim deductions related to your new venture.

Another best practice is to keep a detailed record of all business-related mileage. This is particularly relevant for real estate agents, attorneys, and other professionals who frequently travel for work. Maintaining a logbook of your mileage and documenting the purpose of each trip can lead to significant tax deductions.

Lastly, it is important to stay informed about the latest tax laws and regulations. The IRS often introduces changes that can affect small businesses, and staying up-to-date ensures that you remain compliant and take advantage of any new deductions that may be available to you.

By following these record-keeping best practices, small businesses, restaurant owners, real estate agents, attorneys, car washes, and laundromats can ensure compliance with the IRS while maximizing their profits through lesser-known tax deductions. Remember, accurate record-keeping is not only a legal requirement but also a strategic move that can positively impact your bottom line.

# Chapter 6: Maximizing Your Profits with Tax Deductions: Case Studies and Success Stories

## Real-Life Examples of Small Business Owners Who Optimized Their Deductions

In this subchapter, we will explore real-life examples of small business owners who successfully optimized their deductions, resulting in significant savings on their taxes. By sharing these inspiring stories, we aim to provide practical insights and ideas for small businesses, including restaurant owners, real estate agents, attorneys, car washes, and laundromats.

1. Joe's Bistro: Joe, the owner of a small bistro, discovered a little-known tax deduction for restaurant owners that allows them to claim a portion of their meal expenses as business expenses. By meticulously tracking his dining expenses and keeping detailed records, Joe successfully claimed a deduction for a substantial portion of his food costs, resulting in significant tax savings.

2. Sally's Realty: Sally, a real estate agent, learned about a lesser-known tax deduction that allows her to deduct a portion of her home office expenses. By setting up a dedicated space in her home for her real estate business and keeping accurate records of her expenses, Sally was able to claim a deduction for a percentage of her rent, utilities, and other related costs, resulting in a substantial reduction in her tax liability.

3. Mike's Law Firm: As an attorney, Mike discovered a little-known deduction that allows small law firms to claim a deduction for their legal research expenses. By diligently tracking his research costs, including subscriptions to legal databases and fees for legal research software, Mike was able to optimize his deductions and significantly reduce his tax burden.

4. Carla's Car Wash: Carla, the owner of a car wash, successfully claimed a little-known deduction for the cost of water and chemicals used in her business. By keeping meticulous records of her water and chemical purchases, Carla was able to deduct these expenses, resulting in substantial tax savings.

5. Tony's Clean Laundry: Tony, the owner of a laundromat, discovered a lesser-known deduction for the cost of maintaining and repairing his laundry equipment. By keeping detailed records of his maintenance and repair expenses, Tony was able to claim a deduction for a significant portion of these costs, reducing his tax liability and boosting his profits.

These real-life examples demonstrate the importance of staying informed about little-known small business tax deductions and taking advantage of them. By optimizing their deductions, these small business owners were able to reduce their tax burden and maximize their profits. As a small business owner in one of these niches, it is essential to explore the available deductions specific to your industry and keep accurate records to ensure you don't miss out on potential tax savings.

# Strategies and Lessons Learned from Successful Entrepreneurs

In the competitive landscape of small businesses, it is crucial to learn from the experiences and strategies of successful entrepreneurs. Their insights can provide valuable lessons on how to navigate the challenges, maximize profits, and take advantage of lesser-known tax deductions. This subchapter aims to highlight some key strategies and lessons that can be applied by small businesses, including restaurant owners, real estate agents, attorneys, car washes, and laundromats.

1. Embrace Innovation: Successful entrepreneurs are not afraid to think outside the box and embrace innovative ideas. They constantly seek ways to improve their products, services, or business operations. By adopting new technologies, implementing efficient systems, and staying updated with industry trends, they can gain a competitive edge and increase profitability. Moreover, innovation often leads to tax deductions for research and development expenses, which can significantly reduce tax liabilities.

2. Prioritize Customer Experience: Exceptional customer service is a common trait among successful entrepreneurs. They understand that satisfied customers are more likely to become repeat customers and refer others. By prioritizing customer experience, businesses can build a loyal customer base, increase sales, and enhance their reputation. Additionally, expenses related to customer satisfaction initiatives, such as loyalty programs or customer appreciation events, can be tax deductible.

3. Invest in Marketing: Successful entrepreneurs recognize the importance of effective marketing strategies. They allocate resources to promote their businesses through various channels, including digital marketing, social media, and traditional advertising. By investing in marketing, small businesses can reach a wider audience, attract new customers, and increase brand visibility. Marketing expenses, such as website development, advertising costs, and promotional materials, may qualify for tax deductions.

4. Seek Professional Advice: Entrepreneurs who have achieved success often attribute their accomplishments to seeking professional advice. Engaging with accountants, tax professionals, or business consultants can provide valuable insights on tax planning, financial management, and growth strategies. These professionals have the expertise to identify tax deductions specific to each industry and guide businesses towards maximizing their profits while minimizing tax liabilities.

5. Build Strategic Partnerships: Successful entrepreneurs understand the power of collaboration. By establishing strategic partnerships with complementary businesses or professionals, small businesses can expand their reach, access new markets, and benefit from shared resources. Joint ventures or referral partnerships can create win-win situations that lead to increased profitability. Furthermore, expenses related to partnership agreements or marketing collaborations may qualify for tax deductions.

In conclusion, learning from successful entrepreneurs can provide small businesses, including restaurant owners, real estate agents, attorneys, car washes, and laundromats, with valuable strategies and lessons. By embracing innovation, prioritizing customer experience, investing in marketing, seeking professional advice, and building strategic partnerships, businesses can maximize their profits. Additionally, understanding the lesser-known tax deductions specific to each niche can help small business owners reduce their tax liabilities and further enhance their financial success.

# Chapter 7: Navigating Tax Deductions: Common Pitfalls and Misconceptions

## Avoiding Common Mistakes When Claiming Deductions

When it comes to maximizing your profits as a small business owner, claiming deductions is a crucial strategy. However, it is important to proceed with caution and avoid common mistakes that could lead to audits or missed opportunities. In this subchapter, we will explore some of the most common pitfalls to watch out for when claiming deductions, ensuring that you can take advantage of lesser-known tax deductions without any hiccups.

One of the most common mistakes small business owners make is not keeping proper records. It is essential to maintain organized and accurate documentation for all expenses related to your business. Failing to do so can result in the disallowance of deductions during an audit. Implement a system to track receipts, invoices, and other relevant documents, either physically or digitally, to ensure you have the evidence needed to support your claims.

Another mistake to avoid is claiming personal expenses as business deductions. While it may be tempting to blur the lines between personal and business expenses, doing so could raise red flags with the IRS. Only claim deductions that are directly related to your business operations and can be substantiated with appropriate documentation.

Being unaware of lesser-known tax deductions is another common mistake. As a small business owner, you should invest time in researching and understanding the various deductions available to you. Some examples include home office deductions, business mileage, startup costs, and even deductions for hiring certain employees. Educate yourself on the tax code or consult with a knowledgeable tax professional to ensure you are taking full advantage of all eligible deductions.

Additionally, failing to consult with a tax professional is a mistake that can lead to missed opportunities or costly errors. Tax laws are complex and ever-changing, making it difficult for business owners to stay up-to-date. A tax professional who specializes in small business taxation can provide valuable guidance, helping you navigate the labyrinth of deductions and ensuring compliance with the latest regulations.

In conclusion, avoiding common mistakes when claiming deductions is vital for small business owners looking to maximize their profits. By keeping meticulous records, distinguishing between personal and business expenses, staying informed about lesser-known deductions, and seeking professional guidance, you can confidently claim deductions that will contribute to your bottom line. Remember, taking the time to understand and implement these strategies will not only save you money but also provide peace of mind during tax season.

# Debunking Myths and Misconceptions Surrounding Small Business Tax Deductions

When it comes to small business tax deductions, myths and misconceptions abound. Many small business owners, including restaurant owners, real estate agents, attorneys, car washes, and laundromats, often miss out on valuable deductions simply because they are unaware of their eligibility. In this subchapter, we aim to debunk these myths and misconceptions, ensuring that you, as a small business owner, are well-informed and can maximize your profits through lesser-known tax deductions.

Myth 1: Small business tax deductions are only for large corporations.
Contrary to popular belief, small business owners are also entitled to a wide range of tax deductions. Whether you run a cozy neighborhood restaurant or a small law firm, there are numerous deductions that can help reduce your tax liability and increase your bottom line.

Myth 2: Only specific expenses qualify for tax deductions.
While some expenses are more commonly associated with tax deductions, such as office rent and utilities, there are numerous lesser-known deductions that small business owners often overlook. For example, did you know that you can deduct expenses for advertising, marketing, and even the cost of attending industry conferences or seminars? By familiarizing yourself with the lesser-known deductions specific to your industry, you can significantly reduce your tax burden.

Myth 3: Home-based businesses cannot claim tax deductions.
If you operate your small business from home, you might assume that you are ineligible for certain deductions. However, this is not true. Home-based businesses can claim deductions for a portion of their mortgage or rent, utilities, and even home office expenses. By understanding the rules and guidelines surrounding home-based business deductions, you can unlock significant tax savings.

Myth 4: Claiming tax deductions will increase the likelihood of an audit.
Many small business owners worry that claiming deductions will trigger an audit from the IRS. While it is true that deductions can be a red flag if not properly documented, claiming legitimate deductions within the boundaries of the tax law is your right as a small business owner. By keeping detailed records and working with a qualified tax professional, you can confidently claim deductions without the fear of an audit.

By debunking these myths and misconceptions surrounding small business tax deductions, you can now approach tax season with confidence and maximize your profits. Remember, knowledge is power, and being aware of the lesser-known deductions specific to your industry is the key to reducing your tax liability and increasing your overall profitability.

# Chapter 8: The Future of Small Business Tax Deductions

## Anticipating Changes in Tax Laws and Regulations

As a small business owner, it is crucial to stay ahead of the game and anticipate any changes in tax laws and regulations that may impact your bottom line. Being proactive and well-informed can help you maximize your profits and take advantage of lesser-known tax deductions. This subchapter will provide you with the necessary tools and strategies to stay ahead of the curve and navigate the ever-changing landscape of tax laws.

Tax laws and regulations are not static; they evolve and change frequently. It is essential for small businesses, regardless of the industry they operate in, to keep an eye on potential changes that may affect their tax liabilities. By anticipating these changes, you can take the necessary steps to minimize your tax burden and maximize your profits.

This subchapter will focus on providing insights and tips specifically tailored to small businesses, restaurant owners, real estate agents, attorneys, car washes, and laundromats. These niches often have unique tax considerations and may benefit from lesser-known tax deductions.

To anticipate changes effectively, it is crucial to stay informed. Regularly monitor updates from government agencies, tax professionals, and industry associations. These sources can guide you through any upcoming changes and help you understand their implications on your specific business. Additionally, consider consulting with a tax professional who specializes in your industry. Their expertise can provide invaluable insights and help you identify potential tax deductions that are often overlooked.

Another crucial aspect of anticipating changes in tax laws is maintaining accurate and organized records. By keeping detailed records of your business transactions, expenses, and income, you will be well-prepared to adapt to any changes that may come your way. Additionally, accurate records can help you substantiate your deductions and ensure compliance with tax regulations.

Lastly, networking with other small business owners in your industry can be a valuable resource. Joining industry-specific organizations or attending conferences and seminars can provide you with a platform to discuss tax-related concerns and share insights with other professionals. By pooling knowledge and experiences, you can gain a competitive edge and stay ahead of any tax law changes that may impact your industry.

In conclusion, this subchapter emphasizes the importance of anticipating changes in tax laws and regulations to maximize your profits. By staying informed, maintaining accurate records, consulting with professionals, and networking with other small business owners, you can navigate the complex world of tax deductions and ensure that your business remains compliant and profitable in an ever-changing tax landscape.

# Adapting Your Deduction Strategies to New Economic Realities

In today's ever-changing economic landscape, small businesses, restaurant owners, real estate agents, attorneys, car washes, and laundromats face unique challenges when it comes to maximizing profits and minimizing tax liabilities. The ability to adapt deduction strategies to new economic realities is crucial to ensure success and financial stability.

As the business world continues to evolve, so do the tax laws and regulations governing deductions. It is more important than ever for small business owners in these niches to stay informed and take advantage of lesser-known tax deductions. By doing so, they can optimize their profitability and maintain a competitive edge in the market.

One of the key aspects of adapting deduction strategies is staying updated on the latest changes to tax laws. This involves regularly consulting with tax professionals who specialize in small business deductions. These experts can provide valuable insights into new deductions that may be available and help navigate the complex tax landscape.

For instance, real estate agents can benefit from deductions related to advertising and marketing expenses, home office deductions, and even mileage deductions for property visits. Similarly, attorneys can explore deductions for legal research, continuing education, and even business-related travel expenses.

Restaurant owners, car washes, and laundromats can also take advantage of specific deductions tailored to their industries. For example, restaurant owners can deduct costs related to training employees, purchasing specialized equipment, or even renovating their establishments to comply with health and safety regulations. Car washes and laundromats can explore deductions for maintenance and repairs, water and energy efficiency upgrades, and business-related insurance premiums.

In times of economic uncertainty, it is crucial for small business owners to be proactive and adaptable. By staying informed and leveraging lesser-known tax deductions, these businesses can mitigate financial strain, improve cash flow, and ultimately maximize profits.

In conclusion, adapting deduction strategies to new economic realities is an essential aspect of running a successful small business, regardless of the niche. By continuously staying informed, consulting with tax professionals, and taking advantage of lesser-known tax deductions, small businesses, restaurant owners, real estate agents, attorneys, car washes, and laundromats can navigate the ever-changing economic landscape and thrive in their respective industries.

# Conclusion: Taking Action and Implementing Tax Deductions for Maximum Profitability

Congratulations! You have now reached the end of our book, "Maximize Your Profits: Lesser-Known Tax Deductions for Small Business Owners." Throughout this journey, we have explored the fascinating world of little-known small business tax deductions that can significantly impact your profitability. Now, it's time to put all this knowledge into action and take advantage of these deductions to optimize your financial success.

As small business owners, you face various challenges in maintaining profitability while managing day-to-day operations. However, by strategically implementing tax deductions, you can minimize your tax burden, increase cash flow, and ultimately maximize your profits. This conclusion will serve as a guide on how to take action and implement the tax deductions we have discussed.

First and foremost, it is crucial to consult with a qualified tax professional who can provide personalized advice based on your specific business needs. They will help you navigate the complex tax landscape and ensure compliance with the latest regulations. By working closely with a tax expert, you can identify deductions that are most relevant to your industry and optimize their application.

For small businesses, restaurant owners, real estate agents, attorneys, car washes, laundromats, and other niche industries mentioned earlier, it is essential to keep meticulous records. Maintaining accurate and organized financial records is the cornerstone of successfully claiming tax deductions. Invest in reliable accounting software or hire a professional bookkeeper to ensure your records are up to date and readily available when tax season arrives.

In addition to record-keeping, staying informed about changes in tax laws and regulations is vital. Tax codes are subject to frequent updates, and new deductions may emerge. Subscribe to newsletters, attend industry-specific seminars, and join professional associations to stay ahead of the curve. By actively seeking out information, you can uncover even more opportunities to reduce your tax liability.

Lastly, don't be afraid to think creatively when exploring tax deductions. While we have highlighted numerous lesser-known deductions throughout this book, there may be unique deductions specific to your business that are not widely publicized. Brainstorm with your tax advisor, network with other business owners, and conduct thorough research to uncover these hidden gems.

Remember, implementing tax deductions requires proactive effort, attention to detail, and ongoing education. By taking action and maximizing your use of tax deductions, you can position your small business for long-term financial success. Embrace the strategies outlined in this book, and watch as your profitability soars to new heights.

Thank you for joining us on this enlightening journey. Wishing you all the best in your pursuit of maximum profitability through little-known tax deductions!

www.ingramcontent.com/pod-product-compliance
Lightning Source LLC
Chambersburg PA
CBHW040324010626
45792CB00024B/2121